SAND PAINTING
For Terrariums & Aquariums

dr. herbert r. axelrod

ISBN 0-87666-626-8

Distributed by Federal Marketing Corp.,
62-70 Myrtle Avenue
Passaic, N.J. 07055
(201) 472-1400
Published by T.F.H. Publications, Inc.
P.O. Box 27
Neptune, N.J. 07753

TABLE OF CONTENTS

All photographs not otherwise credited were taken by the author.
The author wishes to express his thanks to models Mame Green and Louve Woods; and to Agnes Pamela Miller for getting him started.

By the time you have finished this book and made all the simple designs illustrated step-by-step, you will be able to take any goldfish bowl, jar, plastic container. . . or even an old plastic bag, and fill it with sand in an interesting design.

Small plastic containers are available every-where. You can make this small cactus planter very simply. . . just by looking carefully at the photographs from pages 33 through 64. It won't take more than 5 minutes to make! Then visit your local florist. . . get small cacti. . . and you have some very lovely gifts or items to sell at your church or school bazaar!

Be sure to use waterproof colored gravel or the colors will run when you water the cactus.

If you just want something beautiful to look at, you can buy only a few colors of sand. . . then buy some white. . . and color it with food coloring dyes available at most supermarkets.

What is Sand Painting?

There is nothing new about "painting" or "design-making" in sand. The art is an old one and has been practiced by many American Indian tribes for thousands of years. Some of the interesting sand paintings are still utilized in the tribal rituals but, until now, the designs were temporary and almost always the ritual would call for the destruction or defacement of the design.

Now we are able to make designs in small sizes, using many colors of waterproof gravel, and to preserve these designs by constructing them in small, portable containers.

Of course there is nothing to stop you from using large containers. . . or even making sand designs in your own window by glazing the window with two panes of glass!! As a matter of fact, many young people find that it is a lot more fun. . . and much cheaper. . . to make a double-glazed window and fill it with an interesting sand design than to buy shades, drapes and blinds to achieve privacy (and it serves as an excellent insulation).

But sand designing and sand painting are easy and natural. Ever since the first sailor scratched a large S.O.S. on a beach, the art and usefulness of sand painting has increased, until now, when it is becoming a real art.

By following the detailed photographs, step-by-step, you will be able to produce nice designs for your aquarium or terrarium (or your window!). . . and by using your imagination you'll be able to innovate and make designs which you would have thought impossible. YOU NEED NOT HAVE ANY ARTISTIC TRAINING. . . you only need the desire to create beauty.

This beautiful glass hexagon (six-sided) planter terrarium is called Item 9-10K by its designer and manufacturer, Terrestrial Terrariums, Franklin, Wisconsin 53132. This beautiful design is 9" wide and 10" high. Cacti need not be watered too frequently; this has its advantages in preventing algal growth on the wet sand.

What Equipment Do You Need?

Sand painting requires a minimum of investment. Aside from the clear glass or plastic container which will hold the design, you will require sand in as many colors as possible (or white sand with dyes); some plastic spoons which you can get free at most restaurants; a wooden knitting needle or any slender tool that is about 12" long

The old goldfish bowl is an interesting and inexpensive container for sand painting since the design can vary from front to back and from side to side, running in one continuous, flowing pattern.

This young lady prepared her design in this goldfish bowl and planted very delicate, tropical rain-forest plants in the top. She then immersed the container in her aquarium with the top of the goldfish bowl just above the top of the water. The heat from the aquarium . . . and the humidity. . . make a perfect environment for the plants, and the decoration in the aquarium is pleasing.

and has a point; small plastic bags to hold the different colors and to assist in pouring the sand; potting soil; gravel (the kind they use in the aquarium); and some plants if you want to make planters. THAT IS ALL YOU NEED! And, as you can judge for yourself, it won't cost too much to get this material.

There are many interesting shapes of all-glass aquariums manufactured for the use of sand painters. The tops are sealable, making these aquariums suitable for housing small animals as well as delicate plants. Photo courtesy of O'Dell Manufacturing, Inc., Saginaw, Michigan.

This is a MH-3 Mini-Greenhouse designed and manufactured by Terrestrial Terrariums, 9670 South 60th Street, Franklin, Wisconsin 53132. This miniature greenhouse is great for viewing your colorful sandscape and delicate plants. The greenhouse is an all-glass construction, "invisibly" bonded with silicone cement. The special glass is scratch-resistant and will not discolor. The base is molded plastic so it won't rot (like wood). The removable glass roof is center-hinged for easy maintainence and the moisture is controlled by side venting. It measures 12" long, 6" wide and 7" high. It is a stock item and can be seen at many petshops.

Where Can You Buy It?

Almost every petshop, flower or plant shop, variety store or hardware store should be able to supply you with almost everything you need. Getting the sand in a waterproof color is the most difficult part since many "bargains" are available.

Plastic flowerpots are now available for sand painting. The wide top and the relatively shallow depth makes this type of container much easier for the beginner. The designs on the facing page are more difficult since the containers are so narrow and deep, but they are beautiful and very easy to design. See the TFH book *Sand Designing for Terrariums & Aquariums* by Agnes Pamela Miller ($.89) for complete step-by-step instructions on making designs in round, deep containers. Usually you need a potters' wheel and a bent, long-handled ice-tea spoon to place the sand symmetrically in the containers.

These interesting designs were made by the noted authority, Agnes Pamela Miller. Ms. Miller wrote the first book on the subject. It is entitled *Sand Designing for Terrariums & Aquariums*.

The waterproof sand is very difficult to make since it requires waterproof paint or dye similar to that used in automobile finishes. This paint is dissolved in a highly flammable, highly volatile solvent and mixed with the sand in a rotating hopper. It must be thoroughly dried before being packaged. Naturally such sand is more expensive than the colored sand made in a cement mixer with water and vegetable food coloring, which is not waterproof. Petshops sell colored sand for aquariums, so you are sure to get the best quality from your local petshop.

The containers, aquariums, terrariums, goldfish bowls, brandy snifters, etc., are also available at petshops. Very often "leakers" (aquariums with defective sealing) can be purchased at very reasonable prices (usually at 50% discount from the price of a new tank) for use as terrariums. Leakers can be simply repaired with any one of many silicone aquarium sealers.

Many aquarium manufacturers are also making interesting and varied shapes of all-glass aquariums to satisfy the market created by "sand painters." The techniques described in this book apply equally well to any size or shape of container.

Problems You Should Be Aware Of!

While sand painting is itself a very simple and enjoyable art form which is especially suited for kindergarten classes and senior citizens hobby rooms. . . and almost everyone else in between, there are some potential problems (though none are very serious).

If you use sand painting to decorate the bottom of the cactus garden, then the sand is probably of the right size and will not pack too tightly for the roots to get sufficient air. Additionally, cacti require so little water that the water which reaches the lower sand layers would evaporate before it faded the gravel or started to support an algal growth.

ALGAE can be a serious problem. Aquarium hobbyists already know that if they put their aquarium on a window ledge or in direct sunlight, the water will turn pea soup green from the algae growing in the water. The plants growing in the sand, on the other hand, are usually sun lovers and require lots of direct sunlight in order to thrive. How, then, can we water the plants sufficiently, keep the sand-painted container in the sun, and still not have our sand painting ruined by algae growing all over the sand and the glass?

There are two easy ways to prevent this situation. The first is to prevent the water from getting to the sand. This is easy. Either you can make your sand design around a flower pot and just water the flower pot, which was buried inside the sand painting as you made your design, or you can make your sand design with a hole in the middle (in which you will put the topsoil or potting soil) and then pour molten wax over the design so that it is held permanently in place and protected from water getting in. This same waterproofing can be achieved with a plastic layer separating the potting soil from the colored sand. Algicides are also available at petshops.

Old water glasses, apothecary jars and special cylindrical containers make suitable containers for the sand painter.

Cacti and succulents are both slow growing plants suitable for the mini-terrarium. In the design above, an old glass jar has been utilized for the creation of a succulent paperweight. On the facing page, more Agnes Pamela Miller designs in water glasses. . . and in glasses which take a top! The Chinese are accustomed to having a glass of cold tea by their desks all day. These tea glasses are usually covered to keep out dust and insects. If you can find a source for these tea glasses with their covers (see lower left photo on the facing page) you will be able to have a mini-covered terrarium in a glass! A covered terrarium needs almost no watering since the evaporation is minimal.

CARRYING an aquarium filled with sand can be dangerous. Be sure that when you carry any aquarium or terrarium made of glass that you always carry it from the bottom, supporting the weight equally on both sides. It is much safer to place the aquarium or terrarium on a piece of plywood and have two people carry the plywood (like a serving tray) so the weight is evenly distributed all over the bottom.

LOCATING your heavy all-glass terrarium or aquarium is very important. You must be sure that the all-glass structure is placed on an absolutely flat surface. If there is a lump or even a small nail projecting into the base of the glass, the resulting uneven pressure might split the glass, causing a very unpleasant situation. Every aquarium shop has aquarium stands to fit the base of most aquarium-terrariums. They are very inexpensive (cheaper than a table) and usually have an extra shelf, too. It is highly recommended that you use one.

MISTAKES in design are easily corrected as you go along. But should you want to tear your whole design apart, don't try to save the sand for detail work. Very often if you mix all the sand together, you get a pleasing color (usually light brown) which makes an excellent desert scene. . . or, as a last resort, it can be used for filling in the voids behind the scenes.

This large hexagonal planter has many advantages. It can be placed in the center of an area and can be viewed from all sides, at the same time protecting the plants it contains from too much dirt and drying-out. The beautiful owl in the tree sand painting is not difficult at all! Photo courtesy of Terrestrial Terrariums. ——➤

Plastic flower pots are available in hexagonal or circular shapes. Both make excellent containers for the sand painter. The illustration above was made in exactly the same manner as the geometric design which starts on page 23.

Depending upon your planting scheme, the plastic flower pot can be mostly sand (facing page) or mostly potting soil (photo above). You should plan the depth of the sand design before you begin working on the flower pot. Sometimes, using a wax pencil, you are able to sketch the design right on the flower pot or glass before you begin!

THE 5-MINUTE, EASY-TO-MAKE, GEOMETRIC PLANTER

In the photograph above, Mame Green takes us through the design of her geometric planter in just 5 minutes. The equipment she has assembled is:

a—various bags filled with different colored, waterproof sand.
b—a plastic spoon she took home from a hamburger eatery.
c—an antique container she paid $1 for at a flea market.
d—various small plants she cultivated and/or purchased locally.
e—a wooden knitting needle.
f—potting soil.

FOLLOW THE BLACK AND WHITE PHOTOGRAPHS, STEP-BY-STEP, AND READ THE CAPTIONS UNDER THE CORRESPONDING COLOR PICTURES.

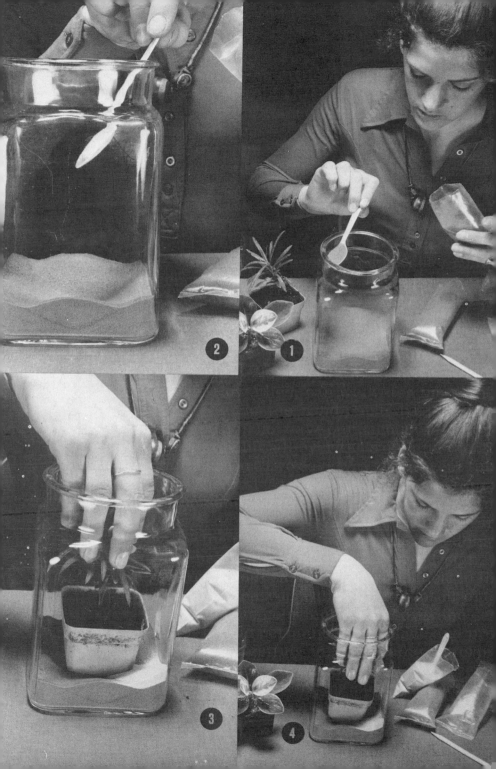

Spoon out the sand slowly, building up the corners. Hold the spoon very close to the corners of the glass but do not touch the glass with the spoon. After building up the four corners with one color, build up mounds in between the corners with a contrasting color. At this stage you can put in the plant, flower pot and all, so you won't waste too much sand (see illustrations 1, 2, 3 & 4 on page 23).

If you decide not to put in the plant at this stage, continue with the design. It is wise not to plant early for if the plant should have to be replaced, the design would be destroyed. Keep alternating your layers of sand between the high corners. . . and the even higher mounds in between. Note that the corners and mounds need not be uniform (see illustrations 5, 6, 7 & 8 on page 26).

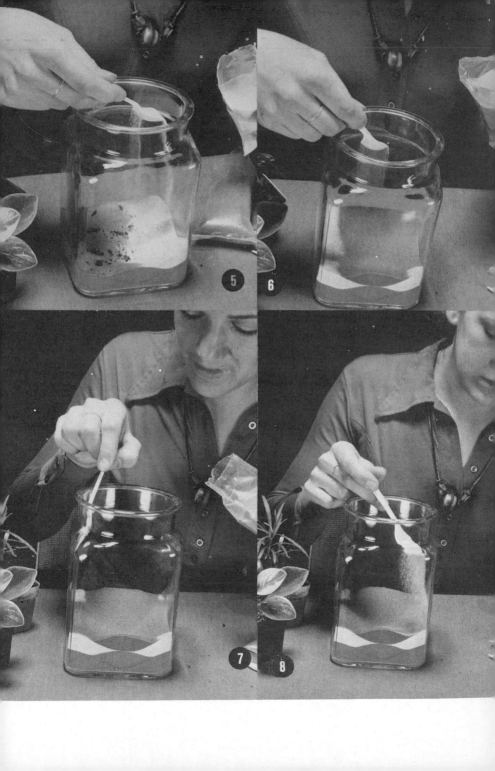

After building up the design with variously colored layers until you have reached a height sufficient for your purposes, be sure that the last layer is dark in color. This helps to hide the inevitable mixing of some soil in with the top layer of sand and it also hides the possible wetness of the sand should your seal between the sand and the soil leak (see illustrations, 9, 10, 11 & 12 on page 27).

After you have made your sand design, add an inch or two of potting soil to the center of the container. Note that the center is lower than the sand level at the walls of the container. Then remove the plant from the pot, free the roots of most of the soil, and plant in the container (see illustrations 13, 14, 15, 16 & 17 on page 30).

After you have added a few inches of soil loosely to the container and have removed most of the soil adhering to the roots of the plant, put the plant in and pack the soil firmly (not too tight) all around the plant. Be sure to get instructions on how to properly plant the particular species you are dealing with. Your planter with its unique sand design is completed. Congratulations!

YOUR OWN AQUARIUM BACKGROUND

Every aquarium should have a beautiful background. This is a really easy design. Use two layers of contrasting colors and poke into it with your knitting needle. Follow the detailed instructions starting on the next page.

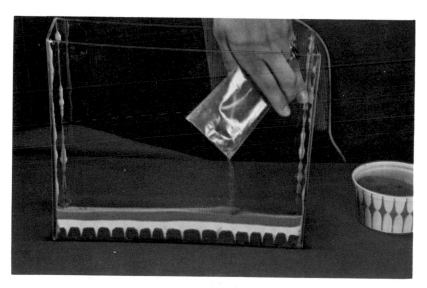

Aquarium Background

This next series of photographs will take you, step-by-step, through the design of an aquarium background. This same technique can apply to any large, flat scene. It is the same kind of design that can be used in a window. Pour even layers for this technique. To start the designs shown here see illustrations 22-26 on page 35.

22—The aquarium background color should be carefully chosen. You do not want the background to conflict with the beautiful colors of your fishes.

23 & 24—Use a piece of glass almost the same size as the back of the tank. Using silicone cement, glue in the piece of glass so it isolates the back inch or two from the rest of the aquarium. The aquarium used in this design is a very flat one to begin with, but it shows how easily this technique can be mastered even in tight areas.

25—Lay in a layer of about one inch of color. Use a dark color for the base line. Make sure the sand is evenly laid; use your spoon to level the sand. The more level the sand, the more effective this particular design will be. However, don't be discouraged. . . it doesn't really have to be perfectly level. Beginners might use a piece of masking tape on the outside. . . or even a straight line ruled on the glass with a glass-marking wax pencil. . . as a level to follow.

26—As soon as the dark layer is level, add a lighter level of sand. Pour the sand gently from a small plastic bag so that you do not disturb the level of the previously laid base layer of colored sand.

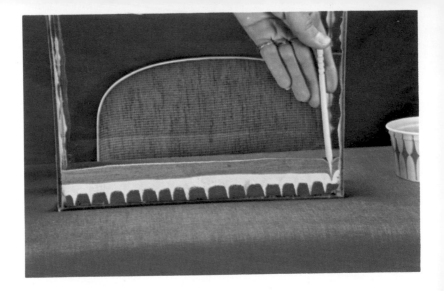

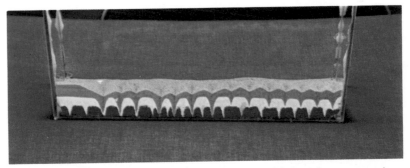

The indentations are made by regularly spaced jabs of your wooden knitting needle. It is very important that you learn how to make these jabs so that the upper layer of sand will filter into the lower layer. Turn to page 42 now and check the proper procedure for using your wooden knitting needle.

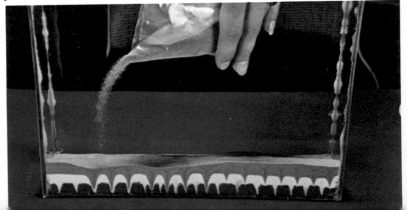

It is most important that you keep the sand level. If you pour in too much sand at one point, use your spoon to remove the sand and level it out again.

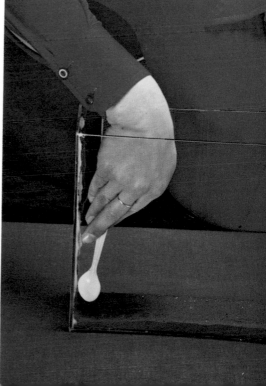

27—Since it is of the utmost importance that you keep the level of each layer of sand as even as possible, you must pour the next higher level very gently so as not to disturb the level you previously laid.

28—Sprinkle the sand gently from a small plastic bag so you can control the flow and intensity with which the sand will fall. Keep sprinkling, adding enough sand to make it twice as thick as the previous layer.

29—As soon as you have jabbed the design between the two layers of sand, you must add additional sand to level out the irregularities you caused by withdrawing the needle in a backward direction.

30—Now that you have done one side of the design, perhaps you might want to make a design in the rear. Illustration 29 shows the design made by jabbing the wooden knitting needle completely through the sand, with the point of the needle touching the glass.

31—This photograph shows the effect of jabbing the needle more shallowly than that in picture 29. Note the furrow caused by moving the wooden knitting needle backward before it is withdrawn from the sand.

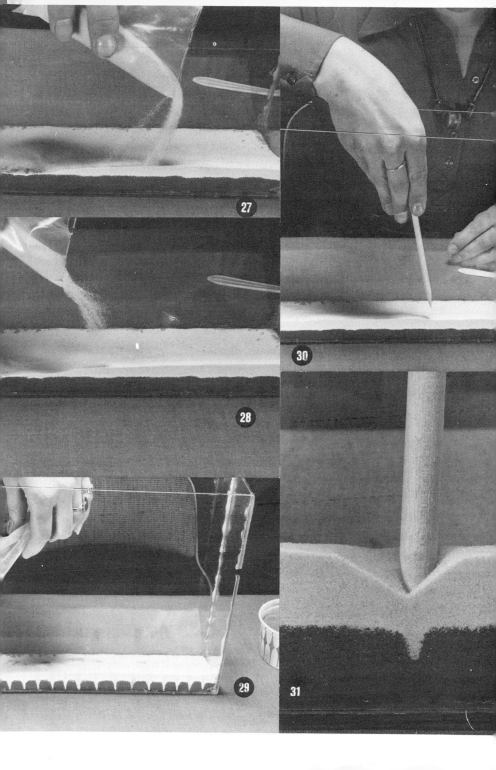

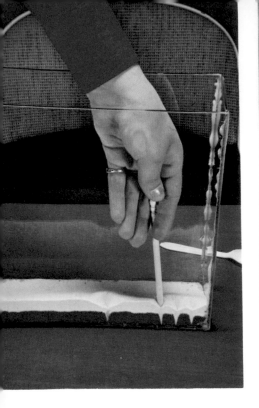

The design you make can vary with your own taste. This is a very simple design, but you can visualize that different colors of sand, differing depths of sand and differing jab lengths all will affect the final design.

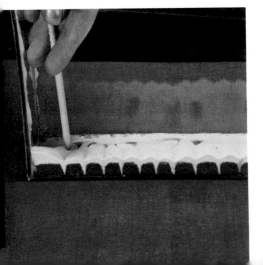

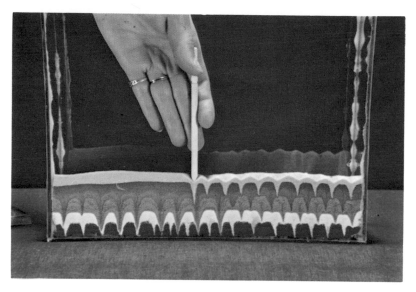

This interesting design shows varying effects with staggered inoculations of different colors. Note that the lowest layer of jabs is "out of step" with the second layer, but the third layer lines up with the first layer of jabs. There is no end to the combinations of designs you can make.

Making Proper Use of the Wooden Knitting Needle

You can use a wooden knitting needle. . . or a pencil, for that matter. . . to make inoculations into sand layers. This same needle is used for additional designs as you get more experience, so get a good one. . . as long as possible for deep work, and a short one for precision work. In A, above, you will find that the needle has been inserted about one inch into the sand just barely touching the outside glass. The needle is withdrawn (in B), so that a furrow is formed. If you had pulled the needle straight out you might not have had the top layer of sand inoculate the bottom layer as cleanly and clearly as this. You can see, in C, the exact way to hold the needle to achieve this effect. After the entire design is jabbed into the sand, your top layer will be a series of furrows. To rid yourself of the furrows before you lay the next layer of sand, add the same color as in D, and add enough to make the whole thing level again. Thus in E an additional layer of sand has been added to hide the furrows and leave it level for the next layer of sand. . .and for subsequent inoculation of that layer. PRACTICE THIS TECHNIQUE A FEW TIMES BEFORE YOU CONTINUE. If you have trouble in making uniformly spaced jabs, then use a ruler and mark the points off on the outside of the glass (use masking tape).

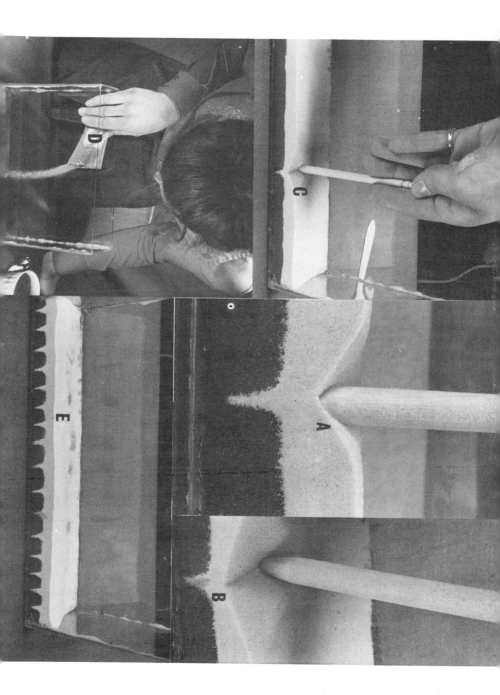

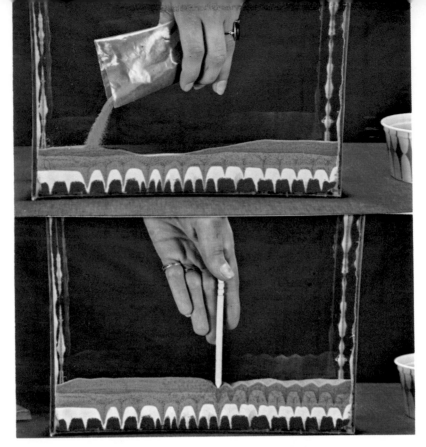

Continue the sand technique as deep or as high as you wish.

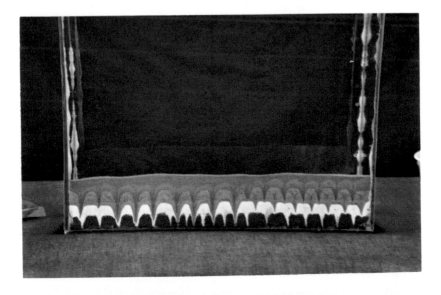

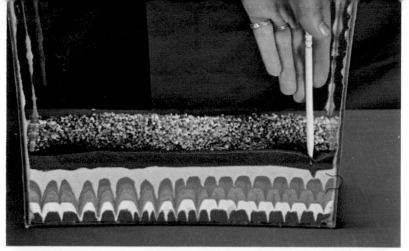

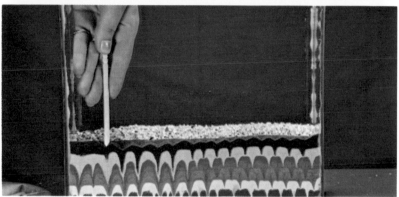

To save sand, use aquarium gravel in the back of the partition.

32—This is the closeup to help you master the technique of jabbing, or sand inoculation. The needle can be inserted either very close to the glass as shown here, or farther away as shown on page 42. The use of the point against the glass is to make a very sharp design.

33—Using the sharp point enables us to bring the sand inoculation right to the tip of the next lower level of sand. If you pushed too far you would have destroyed the level of the first layer. Notice that the two previous jabs in this illustration went a bit too deep and the level is not exactly level.

34—By using the sharp point of the needle against the glass you are able to insert an inoculation inside a previous inoculation, as is shown here. This is a very valuable technique, of course, but it all requires prior planning so you will have made the previous inoculation wide enough for the new inoculation to fit inside it.

35—Of course there is nothing stopping you from making these newer inoculations wide, too, so that other layers might be inoculated through them all the way to the bottom layer. Using different thicknesses of wooden knitting needles would be helpful, but this is not necessary if you practice widening the inoculation by moving it slowly from side to side.

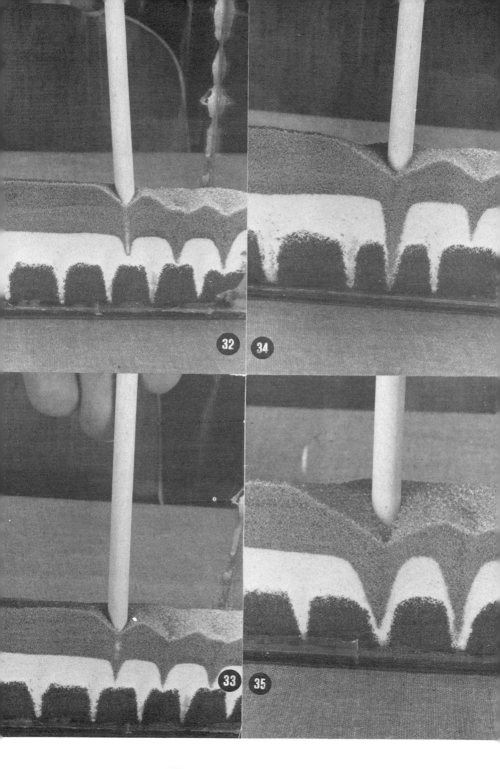

32 34

33 35

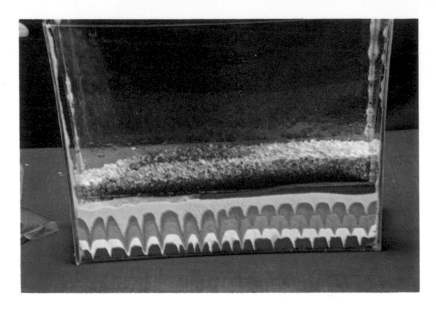

The upper photograph shows the aquarium being separated from the sand background. The sand should not be so high that it covers the design! It is even possible to make the aquarium on one side and a terrarium on the other side with plants growing behind the scenes!

If you want to make a terrarium on top of your aquarium background, just add sand, or topsoil, on top of the design and plant your plant. Or, should you want the terrarium in front of the design, add soil to the front of the sand painting, and put your plant there.

36—As you go from color to color and from one layer of sand to the next, you must always leave the previous layer of sand in as level a condition as possible. This always means adding more sand to hide the furrows left by the backward withdrawal of the knitting needle.

37 & 38—The depth to which you jab the needle determines the depth to which the upper layer of sand will inoculate into the lower level. Making very short jabs makes interesting contrast to some of the deeper jabs.

39—Using the thinner needle, you can make deeper inoculations, trying to get them into the middle of the previous inoculation. This requires a little bit of skill so that the inoculations are uniform and centered.

40—This illustration shows the effects of different jab lengths and of different intervals between jabs.

41—This technique might even work well in baking a marble cake! They use it for making fancy Italian ice creams!

42—You can start your third layer with any color and make it any depth, but the more consistent you are, the more appealing will be your design. In any case, be sure to level the sand after you have finished any particular color.

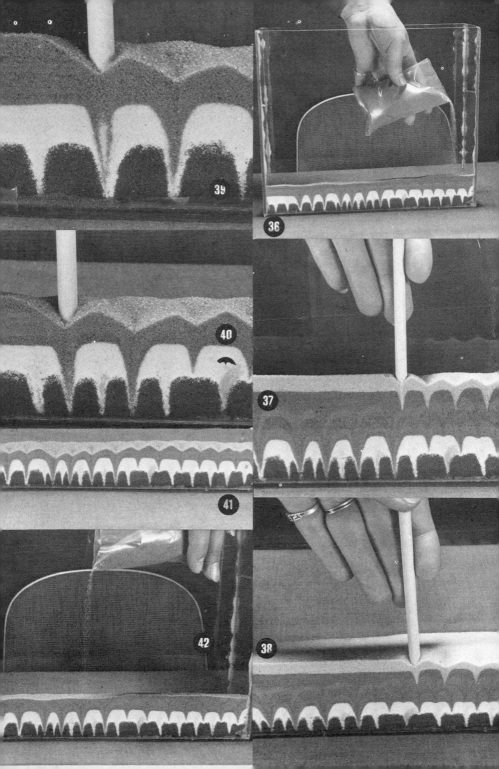

At this stage the design may be utilized in various ways. This shows the divider being utilized to separate the colored sand (which may not have been waterproof) from aquarium gravel in which a water plant has been placed. The lower photo shows that even if the top layer of sand is four inches deep, it is still possible to make a design with the needles.

When planting the terrarium part of the design in this aquarium background mode, you should remove the plant from its container and leave the dirt packed around the roots. Then just place the plant in position on top of the sand and add more aquarium gravel to hide the soil. Then, by completing the design in the sand, or just by adding more colored sand, you can reach the same level on both sides of the partition, thus obscuring the seam between the two types of sand (sand and gravel).

43—Sometimes it might be wise to check the waterproof partition you have just constructed. The best way to do this is, of course, before using any sand. But the cement takes about 24 hours to really be set and you might not have the patience! So test the partition by adding water on one side and see if it percolates to the other side. If it does, you'll have to take out all the sand, dry out the tank and look for the leak! If you used silicone cement on both sides of the partition you should not have any leaks.

44 & 45—Keep adding sand on one side of the partition and aquarium gravel on the other, step-by-step. You don't want to run out of material and ruin your design. Save enough colored sand to be able to level out the previous jabbings.

46—Once you have reached the proper level for whatever purpose you had in mind, bring both levels of sand and gravel to the same point. Then test to be sure that the height of the plant is compatible with your design.

47—Then add enough gravel to bury the plant up to the crown of the roots, while at the same time adding colored sand to maintain the same level. It is much easier to remove aquarium gravel if you built the design too high, but then your design might hide an interesting part of the plant.

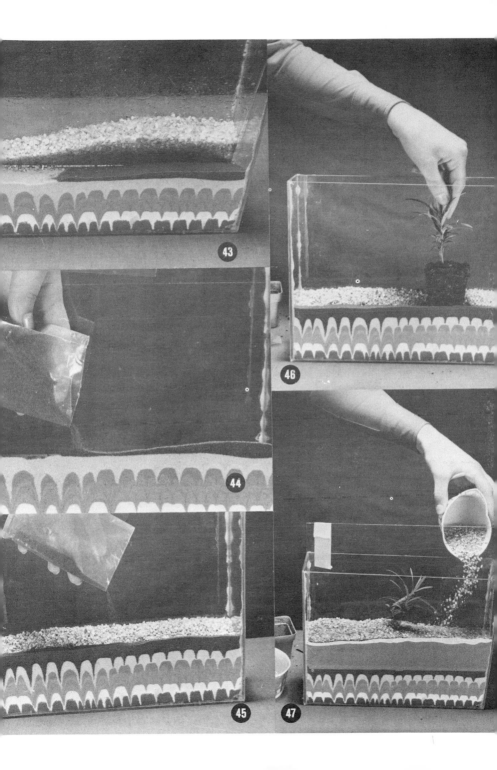

If you are running short of colored sand, you can make a veneer of the colored sand by putting in a glass pane only ¼" from the front glass. Fill this ¼" with colored sand, then add gravel in back of it and gently remove the glass. Plastic plants (for the aquarium, too) can be mixed with living plants.

The partition separating the colored sand pattern from the aquarium gravel can have many uses. It is possible to put plants. . . or anything that is small enough to fit into the area. . . in a display with a sign showing how much it costs. This $50 bill setup was made to show how much it cost for the complete aquarium setup, colored sand, extra glass, heater, pump, filter, aquarium fishes and plants!

48—In finishing off your design, you must make it compatible with the sand or gravel on the other side of the partition. Often you may find it necessary to add several inches of the top color, and you might then find that the flat underlayer is unsightly. It is not too difficult then, at this stage, to insert your wooden knitting needle very deep into the top layer and still complete satisfactory inoculations.

49—The only limit to how deep you can inoculate is the length of your knitting needle. Obviously, the longer the better for deep jabs like the one shown here.

50—After you have completed your design on both sides, level both sides so they appear as one continuous surface. More plants can be added either in front, behind or on top of the design.

51—This is what the design looks like from the front of the aquarium. Of course no gravel was added above the first inch. The aquarium plant is located in front of the sand painting, while the terrarium plant is growing in the sand design and extending above the water line.

48

49

50

51

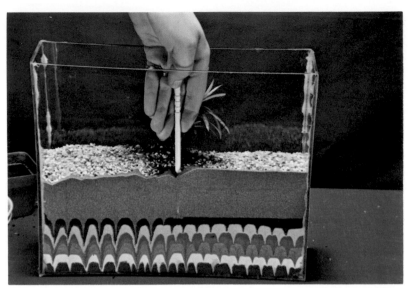

You can compare the profile of the next-to-the-top layer of sand with the half which has been perforated. Perhaps your taste might preclude you from going to the trouble of making sand designs in that particular layer. In any case, even with a short needle and limited space, we are still able to adjust our design to suit our needs.

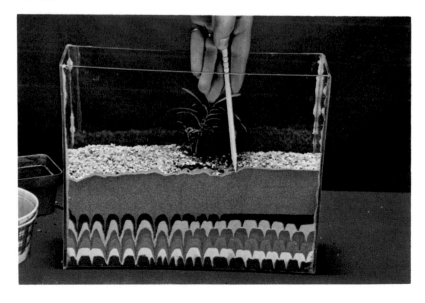

Mame Green finished both designs in about 12 minutes of actual working time. As she worked, the accompanying photographs were taken, step-by-step, so that every point in the construction of these two designs would be clearly illustrated. You, too, can make these two designs now that you have this book to follow.

Directions for Planting

There is no mystery involved in planting a terrarium.

The sand designed terrarium is planted in the same way as other terrariums, with one exception. You should seek to have a minimum amount of moisture reaching the design in order to keep the design in its original state. To achieve this, you may cut a piece of clear plastic film (such as found in plastic kitchen wrap or plastic bags) to fit over the top of the sand design. You simply add the soil mix and then the plants over this film!

MATERIAL LIST FOR PLANTING AND CARING FOR YOUR TERRARIUM

1. Potting soil
2. Crushed coarse charcoal (activated, from garden centers or pet shops)
3. Vermiculite
4. Sharp (or building) sand
5. A container for mixing
6. Plastic film to fit over the sand design
7. Small water sprayer
8. Liquid algicide to prevent algae growth (from garden centers or pet shops)
9. Knarled pieces of wood, decorative rocks, and pebbles.

SOIL PREPARATION

There are many prepared soil mixes for terrariums or for potting plants on the market which may be used. They can be found wherever plant supplies are sold: nurseries, garden centers, plant shops, hardware stores, and variety stores.

The mixture you buy should indicate that the soil is sterile.

You can also make up your own mix.

If there is good loamy soil in your garden, you may use it if you sterilize it as follows. Dampen it slightly and put it in a baking pan. Put this in the oven for about 45 minutes at 175 degrees. Be certain not to let the temperature go above 200 degrees and do not keep the baking pan in the oven longer than 45 minutes or you could alter the soil structure. The idea is to kill the harmful bacteria and retain the good.

Mix four parts of the sterilized soil with one part sharp sand, one part vermiculite, and ¼ part crushed charcoal. (Use activated charcoal from a garden or pet shop, not the type of charcoal used to cook the weekend patio hamburgers.) Vermiculite is available at the same stores that sell potting soil. The sharp sand or building sand may be purchased at a local building supply house. White play sand is too fine for use here; a coarser brown sand is more ideal.

For cactii and other succulents use one part sterilized soil (or commercial potting soil), one part sand, and one part vermiculite.

Spoon the dry soil mixture into the terrarium carefully until there is a layer about 1½ to 2 inches thick. Take the plants and place on top of this soil layer. Add enough soil to cover the roots and hold each plant upright in the container.

Add decorative pebbles or small rocks or even dried and twisted pieces of driftwood as landscaping. It will add more interest to the finished product. All of these materials may be found at most garden shops, florists, or nurseries. Pet shops are also excellent sources for these materials.

Select the plants best suited for the situation. If you want the sand design to dominate the scene, add dried or plastic plants to the top of the terrarium. Plastic plants have an anchor base (see photo above), while living plants must be made a part of the design and can hardly be added as an afterthought.

DECORATING YOUR GOLDFISH BOWL

Almost everyone has an old goldfish bowl someplace; if not, get one from your petshop and discover what a wonderful planter it will make. . . and so easy to design. Model Mame Green puts in her base color and adds green to make some grass.

Mount Fuji in a Goldfish Bowl

This looks like a hard design, but it only took Mame Green 15 minutes. Get a goldfish bowl from your local petshop and pour in the base sand.

1—Put in your base layer of sand. It should be about one inch thick. It can easily be leveled by just shaking it back and forth in the goldfish bowl until it is perfectly level. Using brown sand as a base makes it look like earth.

2—Once you are sure it is perfectly level, place it on a level surface for the addition of the next layer.

3—The next layer will eventually also be a full inch thick, but start by just adding ½ inch of sand. Since we want to imitate grass, this layer may be a green color, though in the fantasy of sand painting almost any contrasting colors are useful.

4 & 5—Visualize exactly how you intend to make the design. Once you reach this point it is impossible to change and have anything that is useful and artful. You are now about to make grass (see illustrations 6-9 on page 70).

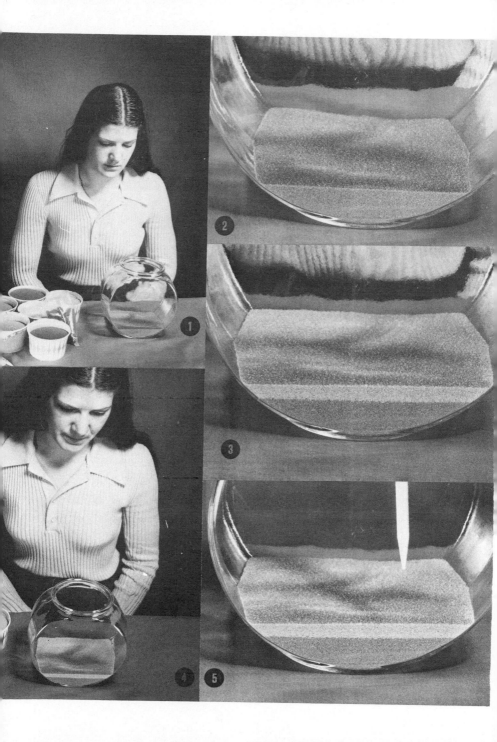

Jabbing the green sand into the brown will produce grass-like tufts. The point here is to make the jabs uneven with different depths and different widths. After jabbing, you can level the sand by revolving the goldfish bowl.

Then add black sand in the middle of the design. Make it as high and pointed a mound as possible. Then cover the mound with a thin layer of white. The black will be the mountain and the white will be the snow. Jab the white into the black to make the effect shown. (See illustrations 9-15 on page 71).

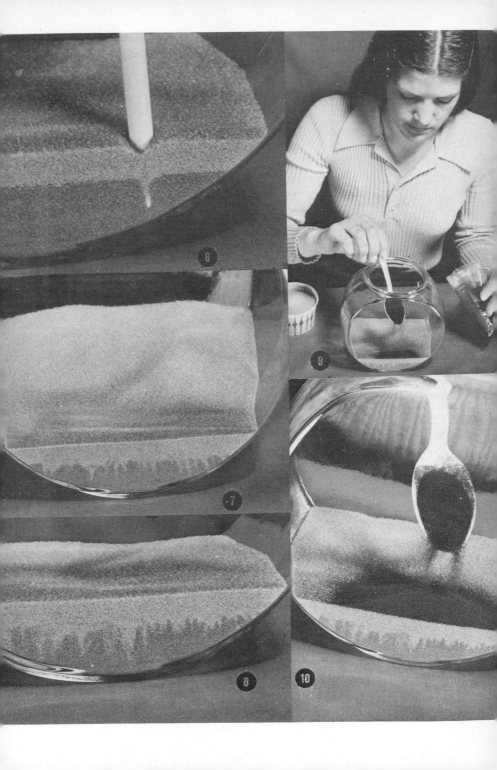

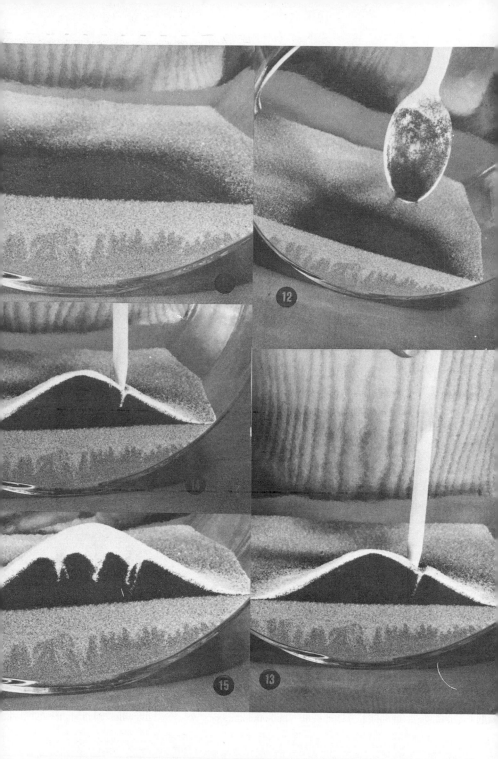

After the center mountain is made, add black sand to the sides, using your spoon, and making it at a different level than previously. Then add white sand as you did before. (See illustrations 16-21 on page 74).

Then add blue for the sky background. Add it slowly and gently, using your small plastic spoon until you have covered the design about one inch deep. Now direct your attention to the sides and back of the goldfish bowl. Start by adding black for more mountains. (See illustrations 22-27 on page 75).

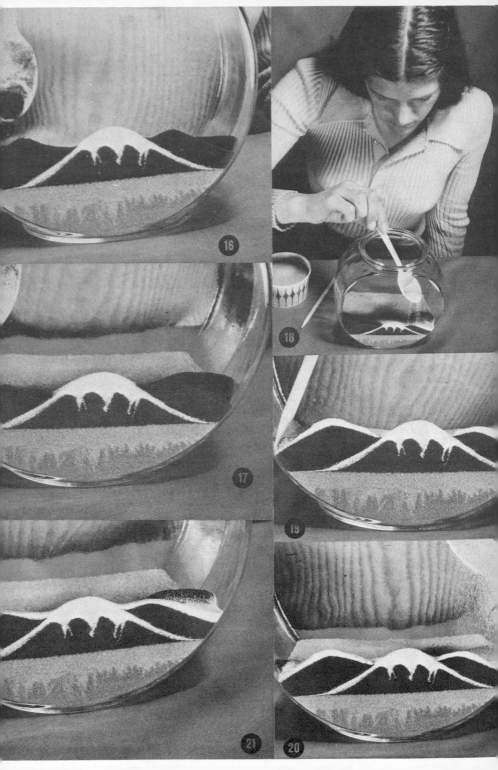

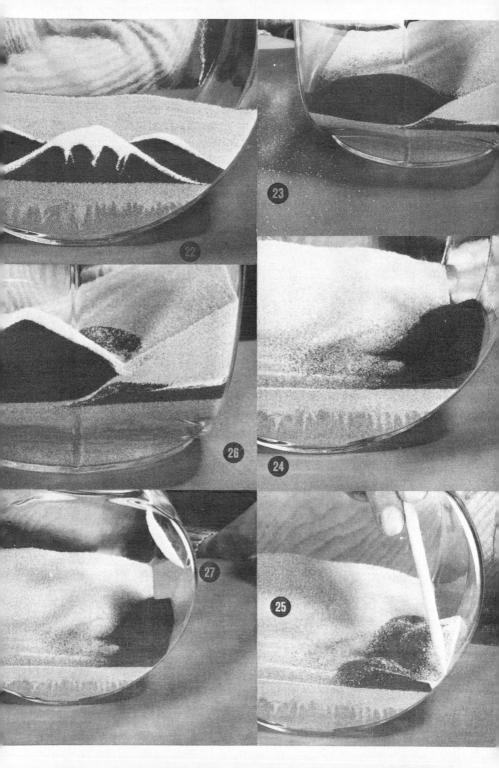

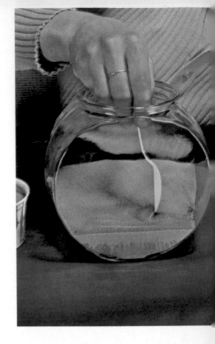

Making the sides and back are merely repeats of making the front. Make the mountain in black, adding the black sand gently from the spoon so it falls into a high mountain. This can be done on both sides and back at this time.

Then add white to make the beautiful snow on top of the mountain. You have to be very careful when handling the design at this stage that you don't jar the goldfish bowl and ruin the mountain! If you do just add more black. Only one side and the front are done in the photos so you can appreciate the slopes of the sand.

28—In case you do not want the goldfish bowl to have a design all around it, you can fill the back with aquarium sand, vermiculite or any material suggested on page 62.

29—Fill the back of the design carefully so you do not spoil the design. Use your hand or the small plastic spoon until the gravel is at the same level as the sand.

30—You can also add rocks or pieces of wood to the scene if you care to. The idea of adding gravel is to plant the goldfish bowl either with an air plant (cactus or succulent) or with a tropical plant immersed in the aquarium.

31—Now direct your attention to the front once again and prepare to add some birds to the sky. By making small mounds of black sand in two areas, you can jab them into the blue and make birds.

32—This closeup shows just how the bird is formed from the small mound of black sand and the shallow insertion of the knitting needle.

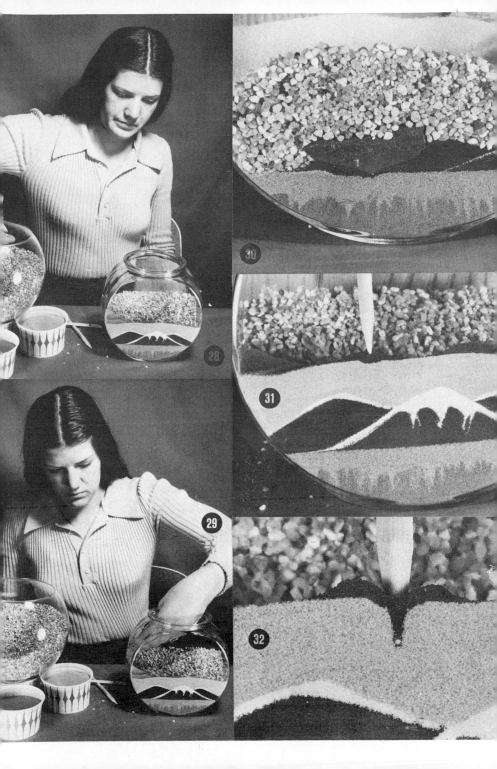

The moment of decision! Should you make a design around all four sides, or just two faces of the goldfish bowl? Once having decided, add black sand to the top of the blue, in small mounds. These will then be jabbed to make birds in the sky. (See illustrations 33-38 on pages 82 and 83).

If you decide to make a planter of the sand design, then fill in the back with any potting material suitable for the plant and the purpose for which you intend the design. Add the sand gently with your hand or spoon. Don't ruin the design at this stage with rough handling.

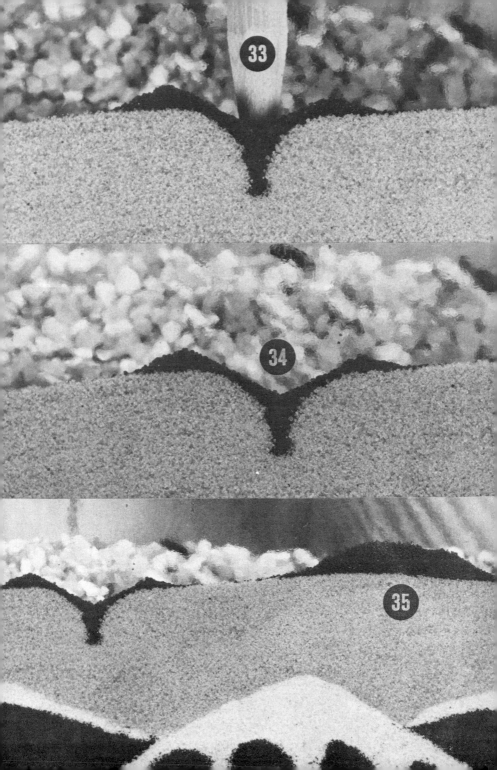

After you have pierced the black mounds to form the birds, you must carefully cover the furrow with more "sky." Then add another inch or two of sky and make another bird. (See illustrations 39-44 on page 86).

Get ready for adding the sun or moon by making a depression in the sand where the sun or moon will go, fill the depression with yellow sand, and then form the circle.

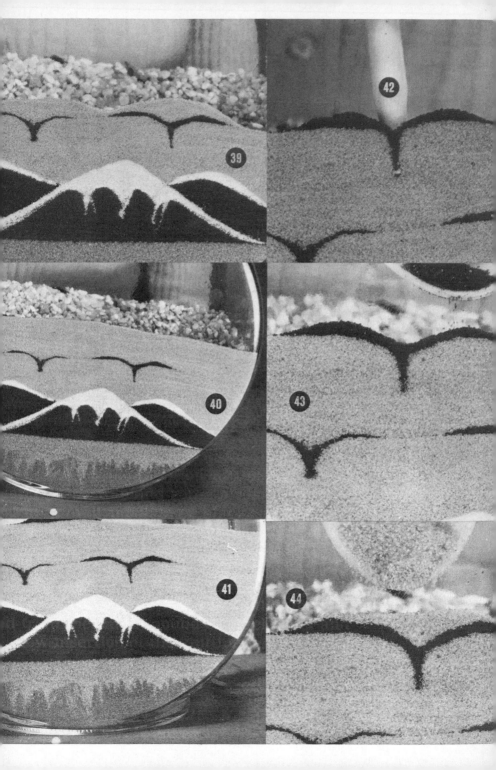

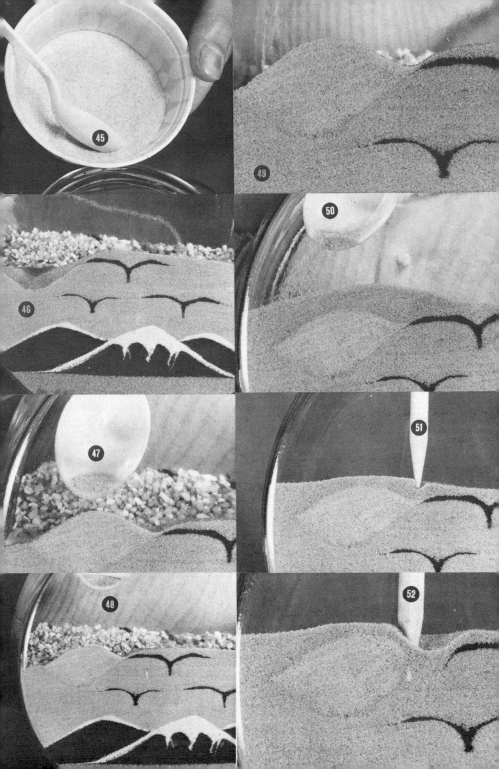

Now we want to put a sun in the sky. Make a depression in the sand (see illustration 46) and fill it with the yellow sand (47) making a mound. Then cover the sun with sky sand (illustrations 48-50) and use the knitting needle to make the sun round. (See illustrations 51-57).

To put clouds in the sky, make small depressions on the other side of the sky and add white sand (illustrations 59-61). Then use the knitting needle to thin out the clouds by mixing in sky with them (62); then cover the cloud with sky-colored sand.

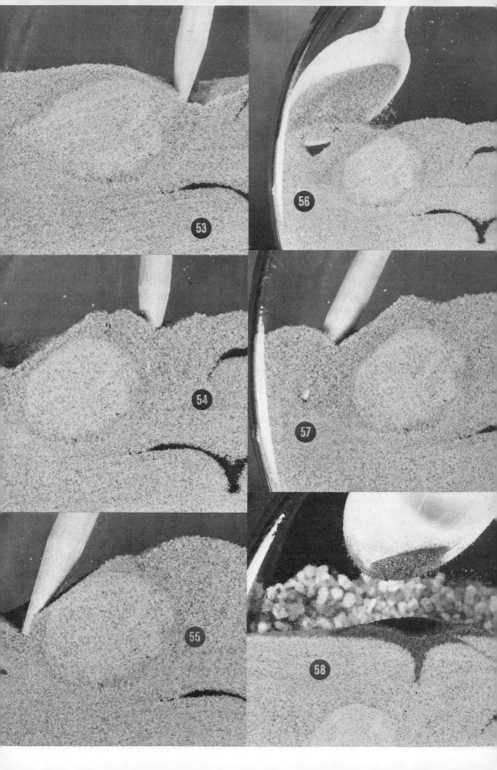

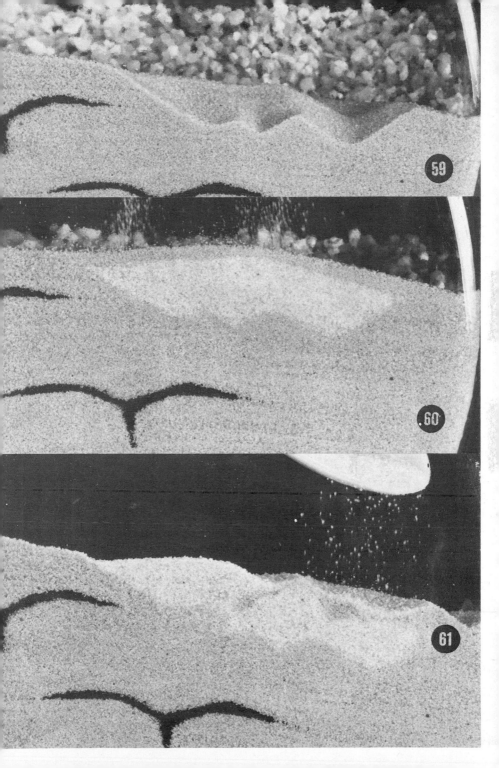

After the clouds have been added you might wish to change the shape since beginners almost always make the clouds too much of a white mass against the background. You can use your needle to make the clouds look more realistic by mixing a little of the blue sand in with the white so it won't be too stark.

After covering the clouds with more sky, you might like to add some more birds. Just make another mound and pierce the sand into the sky. You can use any color. This bird was made red. You can even make black birds with red wings, too.

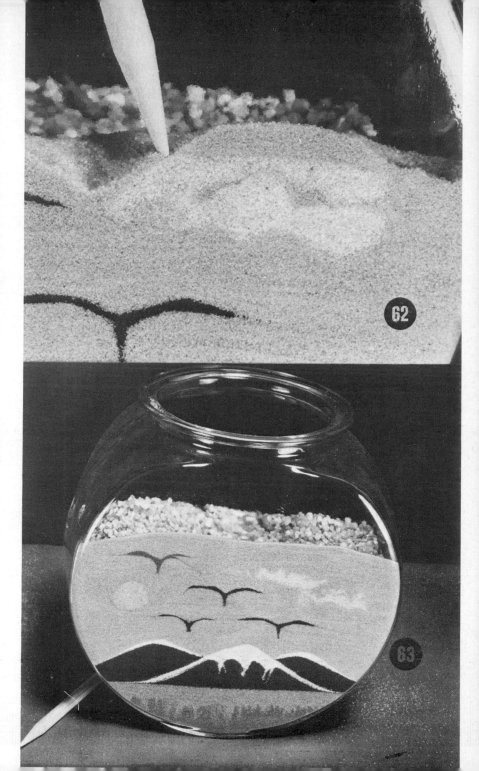

Now your design is almost finished. Just top it off with the remaining sand, plant your selection (a plastic plant was used here) and fill in the open spaces with aquarium gravel (see illustration 63-67 on pages 94 and 95). This design has a beautiful front and an ugly back, but it shows just what we had in mind.

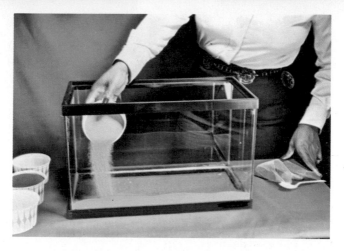

Aquarium & Terrarium Designing

If you were lucky enough to find a "leaker" at your local petshop, you may want to make it into a terrarium. An all-glass aquarium is perfect for maintaining living fishes or small animals along with certain water or rain-forest plants.

68—When dealing with a large aquarium, we must conserve colored sand or it will be very expensive. The idea with this project is to make an aquarium design with living fishes and plants on one side and with the sand painting on the other side.

69—After putting in our base layer of colored sand, we put a contrasting layer on top of it. Then, using our knitting needle, we make "waves" in the sand by irregularly moving the wooden knitting needle in jabbing, sweeping motions.

70—A little practice and you'll have the wave motion technique perfect.

71—Basically you must control the jab motion to displace the light sand into the dark sand as seen in this closeup.

72—Once you have completed the design for the waves, you can add gravel to fill in the back of the aquarium-terrarium. Since the whole back of the tank will utilize aquarium gravel, you might just as well add a huge stack, but be careful that it doesn't disturb your design or touch the front glass.

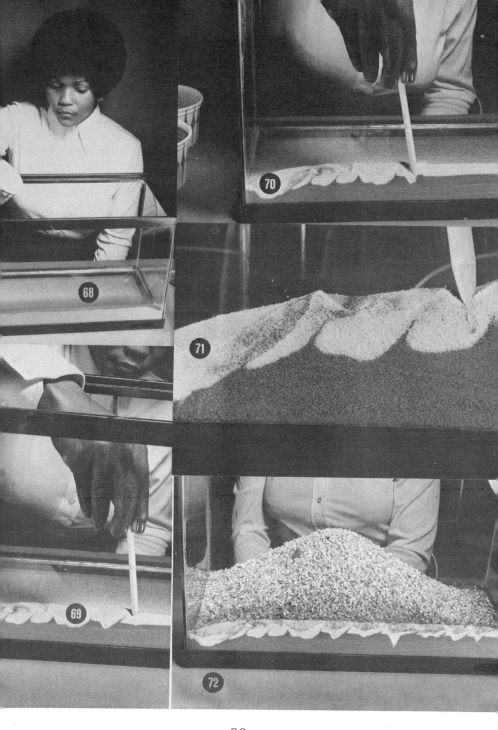

 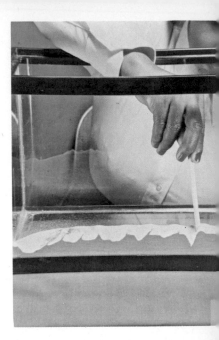

After you have filled the back of the aquarium-terrarium with the aquarium gravel in which the water plants will be grown, you can retouch the waves and add your next layer of contrasting sand. Be sure to add the sand gently and let it fall from against the glass.

As it falls against the glass, push aquarium gravel from the back to the front to support the colored sand design as it grows. This will keep it from collapsing. Now you can add your first mound for the "dead log." Shape the log with your knitting needle. (See illustrations 73-83 on pages 102-103).

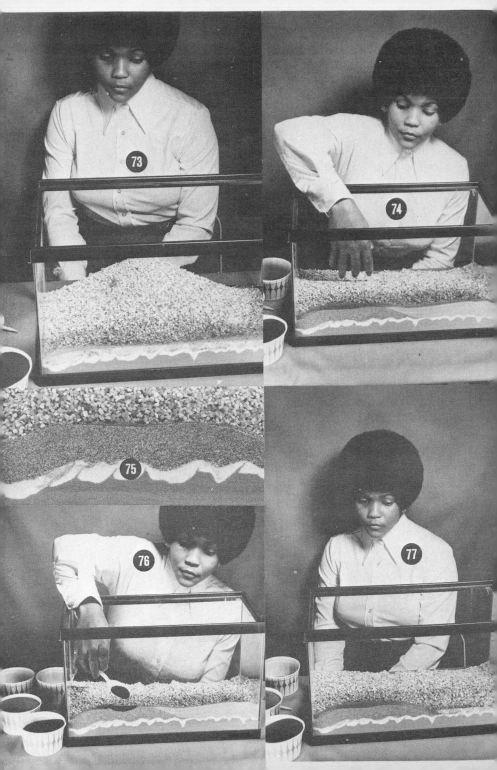

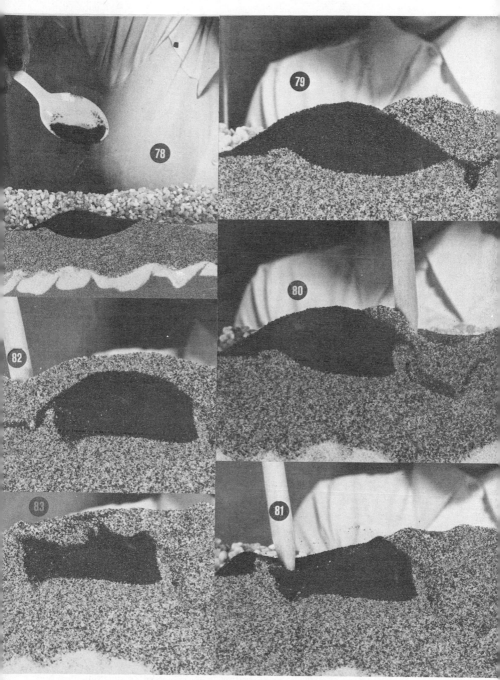

After making the log to your satisfaction, you can add some green sand to another black patch to make leaves on your palm tree. If you want to save sand, use a glass pane with about one inch space between it and the front panel.

The glass pane will make your designing easier. Once you have completed the leaves of the palm tree (which is just like a series of birds in the previous design) stand back and evaluate (see illustrations 84-88 on pages 106 and 107). If it's acceptable, gently remove the glass pane without disturbing the design.

84—In forming the tree, use green and black carefully, with a spoon. Perhaps you might even practice just making a tree in a small water glass?

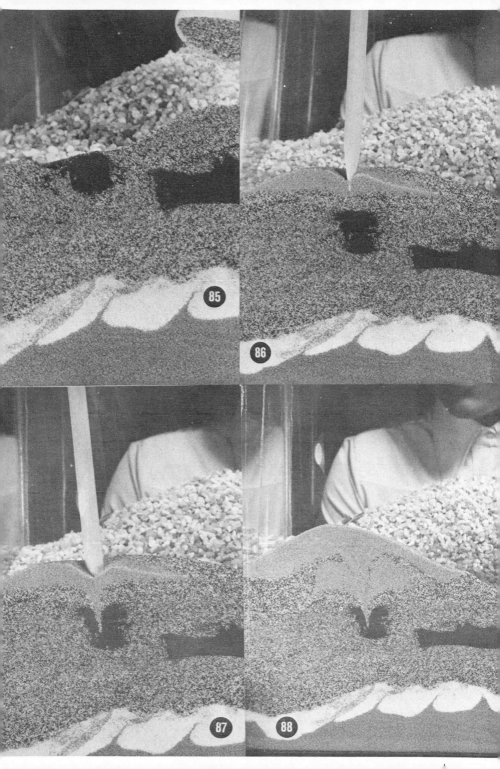

YOUR DESIGN IS COMPLETE! The front looks like an informal beach scene in cross-section. It's not bad for Louve Woods who never made a sand design before, is it? Now Ms. Woods will add her plants. For modeling purposes she is using life-like plastic aquarium plants.

As you can see, sand painting is not difficult. It allows a great amount of freedom of expression and is a wonderful outlet for creative incentive and initiative.

Fortunately, many manufacturers recognized the important market for their products which developed from the sand designing "fad," and they rushed many new, innovative products into petshops, garden stores, variety stores, hobby shops, etc.

Sand painting in antique bottles and jars is a fine hobby, but sand designing terrariums and aquariums can be a money-earning pastime. Once you have developed your techniques, visit your local petshop or garden supply outlet. They might very well be interested in purchasing designs from you to sell. Sand designs are unique, handmade, individual pieces of artwork, and the huge demand for these pieces of artwork has created a shortness in the supply.

On these and the following pages you can see some commercially prepared pieces of sand design. Perhaps these might give you some ideas as to how you can benefit from your new hobby.

The all-glass terrarium has many uses besides being a waterproof all-glass container. Terrestrial Terrariums suggests that this makes an excellent shallow aquarium for turtles, newts, tadpoles, etc. It also makes a most attractive desert scene with miniature cacti and succulents. This design is available in many sizes. . . or your old, all-glass aquarium can be cut down to this size by yourself or your local glazer. Visit your aquarium store and discover what a variety of sizes and shapes is available.

Terrestrial Terrariums makes many styles and sizes of terrariums and aquariums. The advantage of their manufacturing technique is that their all-glass styles are welded together with silicone cement which makes them waterproof. They all have fitted tops and rims of molded plastic.

Garden centers prepare and display many sizes and varieties of terrariums featuring sand designs. Visit your local display for instructions, supplies and ideas. Photos courtesy of Terrestrial Terrariums and Stein Gardens, Milwaukee.

This plastic terrarium was made by gluing some odd pieces of Plexiglas together with silicone cement. Other cements would hold just as well, but silicone makes the bond waterproof as well as being almost invisible if you apply it neatly. Cacti are a favorite for terrariums since they require so little water, thus alleviating the algal threat.

Your local aquarium store will have many different colors of water-proof sand plus many interesting shapes in containers for aquariums and planters. Photo courtesy of O'Dell Manufacturing, Inc., Saginaw, Michigan.

On the facing page is a beautiful miniature greenhouse. This one is decorated with plastic plants and animals, with a few living plants thrown in. Note that this terrarium is placed on a typical aquarium stand which guarantees that the bottom will be secured on a proper, level base. This terrarium would have been much more interesting with tropical plants, a "swimming pool," and perhaps a few tropical tree frogs, lizards, etc. Photo courtesy of O'Dell Manufacturing, Inc.

Not every terrarium must feature cactus, live fish or some other living thing. It is quite possible to use a shallow hexagonal terrarium for dried fruits, flowers and figurines. These make nice centerpieces for Christmas or Thanksgiving tables. They also make innovative gifts. Photo courtesy of Terrestrial Terrariums.

The use of sand designs for aquarium backgrounds is almost self-explanatory. But a further use exists. By placing a fish bowl in the aquarium in such a way that the top of the bowl extends above the surface of the water, you may utilize the heat and humidity of the situation to grow very delicate tropical rain-forest plants.

116

There are dozens of different colors of sand available. By having a stock of these colors, you can make hundreds of other shades by mixing the colors together. For example, by mixing blue sand with yellow sand you get a green sand! By mixing yellow, blue and red together you get a brown sand. Try blending small quantities together and experiment with the colors.

Examples of the types of stands available at most aquarium stores.

The stands come in all sizes and shapes. If you must have a stand
(and it is highly advisable with all-glass terrariums), order the stand
and terrarium together, as some small manufacturers make sizes
for which stands are not available unless they are custom made.
Photo courtesy of O'Dell Manufacturing, Inc.

These photographs (see also facing page) illustrate just a few of the almost limitless variety of sand painting, sand designs, receptacles, colors and plantings which are commonplace today. You can certainly add your own inventive genius to some scene. But be sure to use waterproof sand or sooner-or-later it will fade and discolor. Photos courtesy of Clifford M. Estes Co., Inc., Box 105, Lyndhurst, N.J., manufacturers of waterproof aquarium and terrarium gravel.

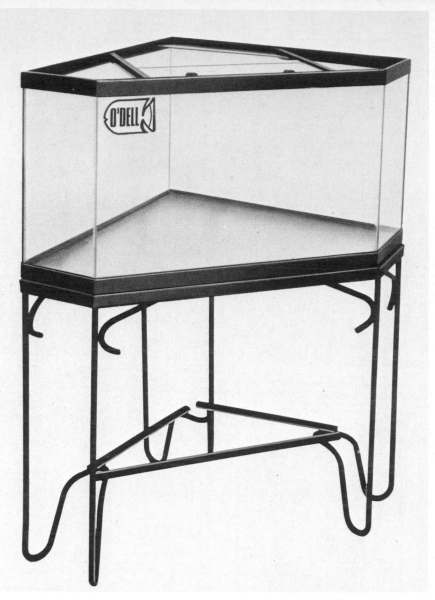

Aquarium shops carry many odd-shaped containers which fit into corners, around poles and within almost anything. Consult your aquarium shop for whatever size terrarium you need. An aquarium and a terrarium are made in the same way by the same people. The advantage of buying your terrarium as an aquarium is that it is guaranteed not to leak. Note the beautiful design of this 5-sided terrarium and its unique stand. Photo courtesy of O'Dell Manufacturing.

This hanging garden is just an all-glass aquarium which someone designed for hanging. It is now an article of commerce and is manufactured by Terrestrial Terrariums, 9670 South 60th Street, Franklin, Wisconsin 53132.

These two pages (see facing page also) are examples of further uses of odd-shaped containers. The large plastic bottle has a removable top, but you could still have made the same designs even if the top didn't come off. Photo courtesy of Clifford M. Estes Co., Inc., Box 105, Lyndhurst, N.J.

One of the newest and most practical inventions has been the KD (for knock-down) Stand. Not only is the stand very inexpensive, but it is easily stored and taken home from the store. . . and it has a bottom shelf which can handle another terrarium or can be covered with a piece of plywood and used for almost any other purpose. Many of these stands are utilized for a television set on the top and an aquarium or terrarium on the bottom. It's the least expensive TV stand on the market! Photos courtesy of O'Dell Manufacturing, Inc.

By the time you have studied this book and made the designs suggested, you will be able to make any of these same designs yourself. Photo courtesy of Clifford M. Estes Co., Inc., Box 105, Lyndhurst, N.J.